Great Kisses

Great Kisses

...and Famous Lines
Right Out of the Movies

TIMOTHY KNIGHT

Harper
Entertainment
An imprint of HarperCollinsPublishers

HarperCollins books may be purchased for educational, business, or sales promotional use.
For information please write:
Special Markets Department, HarperCollins Publishers, 10 East 53rd Street, New York, NY 10022.

Photo credit: Page 84, Photofest

FIRST EDITION

Produced by: Facts That Matter, Inc.
Book concept by: Les Krantz
Designed by: Les Krantz with Kris Grauvogl
Page Composition by: Nei-Turner Media Group, Inc.

Library of Congress Cataloging-in-Publication Data is available upon request.
ISBN: 978-0-06-143889-9

08 09 10 11 12   /RRD   10 9 8 7 6 5 4 3 2 1

Introduction

Ever since John Rice gave Mae Irwin a chaste peck in the 1896 short *The Widow Jones,* the movies have celebrated the kiss. Who can forget the blush of Natalie Wood and Richard Beymer's first kiss in *West Side Story* (1961)? The heat of Clark Gable and Vivien Leigh's passionate kisses in *Gone With the Wind* (1939)? Or the tears of Audrey Hepburn's goodbye kiss to Gregory Peck in *Roman Holiday* (1953)? These images of romantic abandon leave audiences either tingling with anticipation or choked with sorrow. Yet in the thousands of kisses recorded on film since 1896, only a few dozen truly linger in the memory, long after the screen fades to black. Such instances of romantic serendipity, when all the elements magically combine to stir the hearts and minds of audiences— when a kiss is not just a kiss, to paraphrase "As Time Goes By"—are celebrated in *Great Kisses . . . and Famous Lines Right Out of the Movies.*

Over the past several months, I had the enviable job of selecting fifty of the most memorable kisses in film history. Steamy lip-locks alone would not suffice. I was looking for great romantic scenes, i.e., kisses accompanied and enhanced by dialogue that sets the mood and sheds light on the characters. The fifty films I chose span a wide range of genres, from action-adventure to film noir to sparkling romantic comedy. You'll find classics from Hollywood's Golden Age, sentimental crowd pleasers, critics' favorites, and a handful of foreign films in *Great Kisses*—my valentine to the Dream Factory. Enjoy!

Contents

The Adventures of Robin Hood

Not content with stealing from the rich to give to the poor, Saxon outlaw Sir Robin of Locksley has taken an even more precious and rare prize from the fair Maid Marian: her heart. Inexorably drawn to the swashbuckling folk hero with the jaunty smile and playful wit, the ravishing ward of King Richard the Lion Hearted nevertheless plays it cool when Robin scales a castle wall to visit her castle chamber, late one night under a silvery moon.

Robin:

"Very well, then. I'll go. This is rather unfriendly of you, exposing me to my enemies like this." (He nearly slips and falls as she stifles a scream.) "Now let me see. There's a fat old captain of the guard down there with bow legs. I drop on him, that'll bend them outwards. Ah, there's an archer. No, he's too thin. I might miss him altogether."

Marian:

"Robin—."

Robin:

"The very thing! Five men at arms, talking in a group. They'll break the fall beautifully. Goodbye, my lady."

Marian:

"Robin!"

Robin:

"Yes? Then you do love me, don't you? Don't you?"

Marian:

"You know I do."

Robin:

"Well, that's different." (He comes back into the room, takes her in his arms, and kisses her.)

Errol Flynn as Robin

Olivia de Havilland as Marian

Only Arthur looks past the fluttery affectations—the faux air of sophistication and good breeding Alice adopts to fit in with "better people"—to see her as she really is: a gawky and insecure small-town girl of modest means rich in love. So desperate to climb the social ladder she unwittingly pushes her family to the brink of financial ruin, Alice nonetheless has an innate decency and tenderness that's far more valuable to her handsome, old-money beau than social pedigree.

Alice Adams

Katharine Hepburn as Alice

Arthur: "Penny for your thoughts? No, a poor little dead rose for your thoughts, Alice Adams."

Alice: "You came back!"

Arthur: "I didn't go."

Alice: "Why?"

Arthur: "I've been waiting for you."

Alice: "Then you heard—."

Arthur: "Yes, I heard everything. And once more, I—."

Alice: "But I—."

Arthur: "Stop it. Let me finish. I heard a great deal at Mildred's this afternoon."

Alice: "So they did talk about me."

Arthur: "Yes, they talk about you a lot. And I found out one thing. I love you, Alice."

Alice: "Gee whiz."

Arthur: "I love you." (He kisses her.)

Fred MacMurray as Arthur

1955

All That Heaven Allows

Lonely no more, fortyish widow Cary Scott has found a second chance at happiness in the arms of her much younger gardener/landscape architect, Ron Kirby. Their surprise May–December romance has provided ample fodder for Cary's petty neighbors in her small New England town, where even Cary's grown children doubt the sincerity of Ron's affections for their mother. In the restored farmhouse that's their refuge from malicious gossip and resentful children, Ron proves to Cary the depth of his love for her.

Ron:

"You know why I've started to fix the place? I didn't want to say anything until I knew I could make the place livable … for us. Do you understand what I'm saying, Cary?"

Cary:

"Yes."

Ron:

"I'm asking you to marry me. I love you, Cary."

Cary:

"I—I just hadn't thought about marriage."

Ron:

"Why do you think I've been seeing you?"

Cary:

"I didn't think. Can't you see it's impossible?"

Ron:

"No. This is the only thing that matters."
(He kisses her.)

Rock Hudson as Ron

Jane Wyman as Cary

For cynical, worldly wise Los Angeles gumshoe Philip Marlowe, unraveling the labyrinthine web of murder and blackmail enveloping the wealthy Sternwood family is not nearly as challenging as melting the eldest daughter's icy reserve. Although his exchanges with Vivian smolder and crackle with a sexual heat that practically throws off sparks, Marlowe bides his time to make a move on the standoffish beauty, who'll do anything to protect her family's good name.

The Big Sleep

Lauren Bacall as Vivian

Humphrey Bogart as Marlowe

Vivian:
"Are you after more money?"

Marlowe:
"I guess you've got the right to ask that. No, I'm not after more money. I've already been well-paid. I've got another reason."

Vivian:
"You like my father, don't you?"

Marlowe:
"Mm-hmm."

Vivian:
"Why don't you stop?"

Marlowe:
"Remember how I told you I was beginning to like another one of the Sternwoods?"

Vivian:
"I wish you'd show it."

Marlowe:
"That should be awful easy."
(He kisses her.)

Vivian:
"I like that. I'd like more."
(He kisses her again.)

Vivian:
"That's even better."

Breakfast at Tiffany's

Like a chic will-of-the-wisp, she flits in and out of his life, lingering just long enough to leave him wanting her more. Incandescent, with a megawatt smile that could light up all of Manhattan, girl-about-town Holly Golightly dreams of marrying rich, but her true soul mate may be none other than her upstairs neighbor, struggling writer Paul Varjak. The one constant in Holly's restless life, Paul wants to grab onto her and never let go—if only he can stop her from running away, yet again.

Audrey Hepburn as Holly

George Peppard as Paul

Paul:
> "Holly, I'm in love with you."

Holly:
> "So what?"

Paul:
> "So what? So plenty. I love you. You belong to me."

Holly:
> "No. People don't belong to people."

Paul:
> "Of course they do."

Holly:
> "I'm not gonna let anyone put me in a cage."

Paul:
> "I don't want to put you in a cage. I want to love you."

1946

It began innocently, as nothing more than a simple act of kindness. Yet when Dr. Alec Harvey removed a cinder from the eye of fellow railway passenger Laura Jesson, he unwittingly lit a romantic flame that would threaten to consume the both of them, these middle-aged, married strangers. Torn between her allegiance to her dull husband and illicit love for Alec, Laura will suffer the exquisite agony of a forbidden affair that started with one brief encounter.

Brief Encounter

Celia Johnson as Laura

Alec:
"Happy?"

Laura:
"No, not really."

Alec:
"I know exactly what you're going to say. That it isn't worth it. That the furtiveness and lying outweigh the happiness we might have together. Isn't that it?"

Laura:
"Something like that."

Alec:
"I want to ask you something. Just to reassure myself."

Laura:
"What is it?"

Alec:
"It is true for you, isn't it? This overwhelming feeling we have for each other. It's as true for you as it is for me, isn't it?"

Laura:
"Yes, it's true." (They kiss.)

John Mills as Alec

Broadcast News

Uneducated, inexperienced, and woefully ignorant of current events, Tom Grunick is the embodiment of the "Peter Principle," failing his way upward from a local television gig to a network news anchor slot. That he's also effortlessly charming, smoothly seductive, and ridiculously good-looking therefore makes it all the harder for his brilliant, workaholic producer, Jane Craig, to reject him, much to her frazzled dismay.

Holly Hunter as Jane

Tom:
"Do they owe you any time off?"

Jane:
"Fourteen weeks."

Tom:
"I think it's crazy for you to come in tomorrow morning and start a new job. I have a week before I have to get to my new job. Let's get the hell away to some island, fast, and find out how we are together away from this."

Jane:
"Well, I just think … that's an extraordinary proposal."

Tom:
"That's yes?"

Jane:
"That's more than yes. That's you bet."
(He takes her in his arms and kisses her.)

William Hurt as Tom

1954

Carmen Jones

Carmen:
"Where does that leave us? How far apart?"

Joe:
"Only 400 miles."

Carmen:
"Only?!"

Joe:
"You'd come up when I got a pass."

Carmen:
"Boy, if that ain't one on Carmen—love on a pass!"

Joe:
"Carmen—."

Carmen:
"Go to flyin' school. Take off right now. Then lay in your bunk, look up at them pin-up gals. See what that gets you, droopy drawers!"

Joe:
"I got something I want you to see." (He shows her the dried rose she sent him.)

Joe:
"That's been with me all the time (gesturing to breast pocket). Right here, where you are."

Carmen:
"That don't ring so true."

Joe:
(taking her in his arms) "I swear it's true." (He kisses her.)

"*If I love you, that's the end of you.*" Truer words were never spoken than Carmen Jones's siren call to Joe, the straight-arrow military officer who abandons his virginal fiancée to pursue the femme fatale with the bewitching, come-hither gaze. She's like a drug Joe can't quit—this restless beauty who "can't stand being cooped up." And while Joe will put his entire future on the line to be with her, Carmen Jones waits for no man … not even her beloved Joe.

Harry Belafonte as Joe

Dorothy Dandridge as Carmen

Casablanca

He could barely contain his excitement that long-ago afternoon in Paris, when they sat in La Belle Aurore, listening to Sam sing "As Time Goes By." Nothing, not even the imminent arrival of the Gestapo in the City of Lights, could dampen Rick's happiness, for he was leaving the next afternoon on a train bound for Marseilles, with Ilsa at his side. How was he to know that she'd disappear from his life the very next day, only to return years later, when she walked into the Casablanca gin joint bearing his name.

Ingrid Bergman as Ilsa

Humphrey Bogart as Rick

Rick:

"Let's see, what about the engineer? Why can't he marry us on the train?"

Ilsa:

"Oh, darling—."

Rick:

"Why not? The captain on a ship can. It doesn't seem fair that—hey, what's wrong, kid?"

Ilsa:

(fighting tears) "I love you so much. And I hate this war so much. Oh, it's a crazy world, anything can happen. If you shouldn't get away … I mean, if something should keep us apart…wherever they put you … and wherever I'll be, I want you to know that I—."
(He kisses her.)

Ilsa:

"Kiss me. Kiss me as if it were the last time."
(He kisses her again.)

1943

Lying on his back, Salvatore stares at the night sky over his Sicilian village, heartsick at being apart from his first love. If only his life could be more like one of those Hollywood romances he screens at the Cinema Paradiso—one that hasn't been stripped of all its kissing scenes, per the command of Father Adelfio. Then Elena would be here next to him, rather than sent far away by her father, who disapproves of his daughter seeing a movie-theater projectionist. Happily for Salvatore, life occasionally does imitate art.

Salvatore:

"When will this rotten summer end? In a film, it'd be already over. Fade-out, cut to storm. Wouldn't that be great?"
(On cue, it begins raining, as Elena appears, kissing him.)

Salvatore:

"Elena! But when—."

Elena:

"I got back today. You can't imagine the excuses I made up to come here."
(She kisses him as he wraps his arms around her.)

Cinema Paradiso

Marco Leonardi as Salvatore

Agnese Nano as Elena

Facing Windows

For months now, she's been stealing glances at him, the handsome young banker who lives in the flat opposite the apartment she shares with her husband and two small children. He in turn has been furtively watching her, this beautiful woman whose marriage has gone stale. But if not for the sudden arrival of an elderly Holocaust survivor, whose wrenching story of love and loss will trigger unexpected feelings in both of them, Giovanna and Lorenzo might never have met—or found the nerve to act on their long-smoldering mutual attraction, however briefly it may last.

Lorenzo:

"I have to leave in a few days. I'm being transferred to the Ischia branch."

Giovanna:

"It must be a beautiful island."

Lorenzo:

"Yes. But not now. It's always like this. I'm never good at guessing the right timing. A few days ago, I thought this promotion would save me. It's the last thing I want right now. It seems I always get what I want at the wrong time. Everything's fine as long as I'm dreaming of something … but when I try to make that become reality…I don't know how to explain it. Sorry, I know, but, it's just that I … I'd stay sitting on this bench for-ever…even though I know it would never be possible—."
(She cuts him off with a deep, passionate kiss.)

Raoul Bova as Lorenzo

Giovanna Mezzogiorno as Giovanna

1943

For Whom the Bell Tolls

Love was the very last thing on his mind when he joined a rag-tag band of anti-fascist guerrillas, fighting the nationalist forces of Generalisimo Franco in the mountains of thirties-era Spain. Nicknamed "Ingles" by his fellow guerrillas, American explosives expert Robert Jordan knows that he may die fighting the good fight on behalf of "La Causa." What he didn't know was how deeply he'd fall in love with Maria, a radiantly beautiful peasant girl rescued by the guerrillas from execution.

Maria:

"Oh, Roberto, I like—I don't know how to kiss or I would kiss you. Where do the noses go? (laughing to herself) Always I wonder where the noses go." (He gives her a quick peck on the lips.)

Maria:

"They're not in the way, are they? I always thought they would be in the way. (she kisses him) Look, I can do it myself."

Robert:

"Maria—."

Maria:

"Oh, did I do it wrong?"
(He waits a moment, then grabs her in a passionate kiss.)

Ingrid Bergman as Maria

Gary Cooper as Robert

Here comes the groom, with a newly blackened eye, courtesy of the bride he jilted at the altar. Just another very public humiliation in the bloody awful disaster that's been Charles's love life since he fell hopelessly in love with the elusive Carrie—*not* the enraged ex he nearly wed on the rebound. In a London drizzle, the hemming and hawing Brit stops babbling long enough to make a most unusual proposal to the American girl of his dreams.

Four Weddings and a Funeral

Hugh Grant as Charles

Andie MacDowell as Carrie

Charles:

"The truth of it is, I've loved you from the first second I met you. You're not suddenly gonna go away again, are you?"

Carrie:

"No … I might drown, but otherwise, no."

Charles:

"Okay, okay, we'll go in. First, let me ask you one thing. Do you think, after we've dried off, after we've spent lots more time together, you might agree not to marry me? And do you think not being married to me might maybe be something you could consider doing for the rest of your life? Do you?"

Carrie:

"I do."

From Here to Eternity

Caressed by the ocean surf, they lie entwined on a moonlit strip of Hawaiian beach. Here, in the quiet before the storm of the Japanese attack on Pearl Harbor, Sgt. Milt Warden puts his military career on the line to tryst with Karen Holmes, the sexy, infamously promiscuous wife of his commanding officer. It's an atypically reckless, impulsive move by Warden, fraught with grave consequences for both of them. None of that matters, however, in that brief, all-consuming moment when their lips meet.

Deborah Kerr as Karen

Burt Lancaster as Warden

Karen:

> "I never knew it could be like this. Nobody ever kissed me the way you do."

Warden:

> "Nobody?"

Karen:

> "No, nobody."

Warden:

> "Not even one? Out of all the men you've been kissed by?"

Karen:

> "Now that would take some figuring. How many men do you think there've been?"

Warden:

> "I wouldn't know. Can't you give me a rough estimate?"

Karen:

> "Not without an adding machine."

Ghost

They are lovers caught between this world and the next. Yet nothing, not even death, can destroy their bond. True love endures forever. And as Sam bends down to kiss Molly good-bye, their profiles bathed in a glowing white light, he finally tells her what should never be left unsaid.

Demi Moore as Molly

Patrick Swayze as Sam

Molly:
> "Do you love me, Sam?"

Sam:
> "What do you think?"

Molly:
> "Why don't you ever say it?"

Sam:
> "What do you mean, why don't I ever say it, I say it all the time—."

Molly:
> "No you don't, you say 'ditto,' and that's not the same."

Sam:
> "I love you, Molly. I've always loved you."

Molly:
> (through her tears) "Ditto."

Neither shaken nor stirred by Agent 007, the demurely named jet pilot/judo expert Pussy Galore initially informed the super spy that she was "immune" to his manly charms. Yet like so many women before and after her, the formidable Ms. Galore will discover that resisting James Bond is ultimately futile—although she literally puts up a better fight than most of his conquests.

Goldfinger

James Bond:

"What would it take for you to see things my way?"

Pussy Galore:

"A lot more than you've got."

James Bond:

"How do you know?"

Pussy Galore:

"I don't want to know."

James Bond:

(grabbing her) "Isn't it customary to grant a condemned man his last request?"

Pussy Galore:

"You've asked for this (flips him onto his back). Get up."

James Bond:

(pulling her onto the hay) "Certainly. There now, let's both play." (She briefly holds him off before surrendering to his kiss.)

Honor Blackman as Pussy Galore

Sean Connery as James Bond

Gone With the Wind

Widowed a second time, Scarlett O'Hara is sick and tired of mourning dead husbands she never loved. Yet for all her cunning, the ravishing Southern belle nonetheless remains an incurable romantic, pining for the chivalrous, unattainable ideal of Ashley Wilkes—and spurning the advances of her true soul mate, that charming rogue from Charleston, Rhett Butler. He may be "no gentleman," but then again, Scarlett is no lady—which only makes her all the more irresistible to the quick-witted former Confederate gunrunner.

Rhett:

"Did you ever think of marrying just for fun?"

Scarlett:

"Marriage fun? Fiddle-de-dee. Fun for men, you mean."

Rhett:

"You've been married to a boy and an old man. Why not try a husband of the right age—with a way with women."

Scarlett:

"You're a fool, Rhett Butler. When you know I shall always love another man."

Rhett:

(grabbing her) "Stop it. You hear me, Scarlett, stop it. No more of that talk."
(He kisses her.)

Scarlett:

"Rhett, don't. I shall faint."

Rhett:

"I want you to faint. This is what you were meant for. None of the fools you've ever known have kissed you like this, have they? Your Charles or your Frank or your stupid Ashley."
(He kisses her.)

Clark Gable as Rhett

Vivien Leigh as Scarlett

The Lady Eve

Henry Fonda as Charles

Barbara Stanwyck as Jean

Glamourpuss con artist Jean Harrington never met a sucker she couldn't charm out of his dough. And no mark ever looked easier than Charles Pike, the endearingly clutzy, boyishly handsome heir to the Pike Ale mega-fortune. Using all her feminine wiles, and then some, to lure Charles into her shipboard scam, Jean's all ready to play the guileless bachelor for a sap. But it's the con artist who gets conned, when Charles steals her heart.

Jean:

"Oh, why didn't you take me in your arms that day, why did you let me go, why did we have to go through all this nonsense? Don't you know you're the only man I've ever loved? Don't you know I couldn't look at another man if I wanted to? Don't you know I've waited all my life for you, you big mug?"

Charles:

"Will you forgive me?"

Jean:

"For what? Oh, you mean, on the boat? The question is, can you forgive me?"

Charles:

"What for?"

Jean:

"Oh, you still don't understand."

Charles:

"I don't want to understand. I don't want to know—whatever it is, keep it to yourself. All I know is I adore you."

Against the backdrop of Hong Kong's Victoria Harbour, they say their goodbyes. He is off to cover the war in Korea; she will return to caring for the sick at a local hospital. Despite the opposition of her tradition-minded relatives and their so-called friends, the bittersweet, initially clandestine romance between unhappily married American journalist Mark Elliott and widowed Eurasian doctor Han Suyin has prevailed. Now he must bid her a reluctant farewell, on the very hilltop that's long been their cherished meeting place.

Love Is a Many Splendored Thing

Mark:

"I wanted to bring you a present, but there wasn't time. You know, I've never given you anything."

Suyin:

"Oh Mark, what a wrong and dreadful thing to say."

Mark:

"What a nice thing to reply. I have to go now and I don't want you to be sad."

Suyin:

"I won't be sad. Sadness is so ungrateful."

Mark:

"And I don't want you to come down the path with me. I want to look back and see you here."

Suyin:

"I will be here when you come back to me. I promise."
(They kiss.)

William Holden as Mark

Jennifer Jones as Suyin

1955

Love Me Tonight

It takes a certain *je ne sais quoi* for a penniless tailor to woo a beautiful princess. Lucky for Maurice, he has the necessary sangfroid in spades, not to mention a *joie de vivre* that lovelorn Princess Jeanette finds as intoxicating as the bubbliest French champagne. Stealing away from a fancy dress ball at her family's chateau, the princess and her commoner beau seal their l'amour with a tender kiss.

Maurice:

"You don't know who I am."

Jeanette:

"You're you. And I love you."

Maurice:

"But if I—I were not what you think I am. If I—."

Jeanette:

"Whoever you are. Whatever you are. Wherever you are … I love you."

Maurice:

"Cherie?"

Jeanette:

"Maurice?"

Maurice:

"You know what I think? I think I'm mad. And that you're mad. And that the whole world is mad. But I'm the luckiest madman of all. And the happiest. Listen, my beautiful princess. I love you. I love you. And whatever comes tomorrow, love me tonight. Love me tonight."

Maurice Chevalier as Maurice

Jeanette MacDonald as Jeanette

1970

Love Story

Blue blood to her blue collar, handsome Harvard scion Oliver Barrett IV, aka "Preppie," can't catch a break with Radcliffe music student Jenny Cavalleri. The outspoken daughter of an Italian-American baker holds her old-money beau at proverbial arm's length with her snide put-downs. As they walk across a snow-covered Harvard Yard, Oliver issues Jenny an ultimatum of sorts. But if she's chastened, she's not apologetic—for "love means never having to say you're sorry."

Ali MacGraw as Jenny

Ryan O'Neal as Oliver

Oliver:

"Look, Cavalleri, I know your game, and I'm tired of playing it. You are the supreme Radcliffe smartass—the best—you can put down anything in pants. But verbal volleyball is not my idea of a relationship. And if that's what you think it's all about, why don't you just go back to your music wonks, and good luck. See, I think you're scared. You put up a big glass wall to keep from getting hurt, but it also keeps you from getting touched. It's a risk, isn't it, Jenny? Least I had the guts to admit what I felt. Someday you're gonna have to come up with the courage to admit you care.

Jenny:

"I care."
(He turns towards her; they kiss.)

1987

Widowed thirty-something bookkeeper Loretta Castorini had just about given up on love—until she meets that handsome "wolf" in a baker's apron, Ronny Cammareri, a one-handed Brooklyn native as passionate and mercurial as his favorite Puccini opera, *La Bohème*. There's just one tiny complication: Loretta's engaged to marry Ronny's noodle of an older brother. But once she locks eyes with Ronny under *la bella luna*—mama mia, that's amore!

Moonstruck

Nicolas Cage as Ronny

Ronny:

"Why you marrying Johnny? He's a fool."

Loretta:

"Because I have no luck."

Ronny:

(rising) "He—he made me look the wrong way, and I cut off my hand. He could make you look the wrong way, you could lose your whole head."

Loretta:

"I'm looking where I have to to become a bride."

Ronny:

"A bride without a head."

Loretta:

"A wolf without a foot!"
(He kicks over the table, pulls her to her feet, and kisses her.)

Loretta:

(pulling away) "Wait a minute, wait a minute!"
(She grabs him for another kiss.)

Cher as Loretta

Ninotchka

A model comrade, seemingly impervious to temptations of any kind, steely-faced Soviet commissar Ninotchka collides with Western decadence in the tuxedoed form of Parisian Count Leon Dalga. Plying his continental charms for maximum impact, Count Leon gives the humorless, sphinx-like beauty a crash course in the joys of l'amour, which she coolly dismisses as nothing more than "a chemical reaction"—until their lips meet for the first time.

Melvyn Douglas as Count Leon

Count Leon:

"Oh Ninotchka, Ninotchka, surely you must feel some slight symptom of the divine passion? A general warmth in the palm of your hands? A strange heaviness in your limbs? A burning of the lips that isn't thirst, but something a thousand times more tantalizing, more exalting, than thirst?"

Ninotchka:

"You're very talkative."
(He grabs and kisses her.)

Count Leon:

"Was that talkative?"

Ninotchka:

"No … that was restful. Again."
(He kisses her.)

Greta Garbo as Ninotchka

1939

1946

Notorious

Normally the epitome of unflappable cool, government agent T.R. Devlin can no longer mask his growing attraction to boozy, conscience-plagued party girl Alicia Huberman. Drafted by Devlin to infiltrate a neo-Nazi enclave in Rio de Janeiro, Alicia willingly risks her life to redeem her misspent youth—and atone for her father's war crimes. The top-secret government mission briefly forgotten, Devlin relaxes his guard just enough to lose himself in a sizzling encounter with the woman he secretly loves.

Ingrid Bergman as Alicia

Cary Grant as Devlin

Alicia:

> "This is a very strange love affair."

Devlin:

> "Why?"
> (She kisses him.)

Alicia:

> "Maybe the fact that you don't love me."

Devlin:

> (kissing her) "When I don't love you, I'll let you know."

Alicia:

> "You haven't said anything."

Devlin:

> "Actions speak louder than words."

PARTIDA
DOS AVIÕES

1942

B ullied into premature spinsterhood by her controlling society mother, Boston Brahmin Charlotte Vale has finally shed all lingering traces of her dowdy self, thanks to the benevolent care of her psychiatrist. No longer a painfully repressed frump, hiding behind thick, untamed eyebrows and matronly clothes, she's been reborn as a chic New Englander on an ocean cruise—and fallen deeply in love with her fellow passenger Jerry, a suave, cultured architect regrettably trapped in a loveless marriage.

Now, Voyager

Charlotte:
> "I hate good-byes."

Jerry:
> "They don't matter. It's what's gone before."

Charlotte:
> "No, it's what can't go after."

Jerry:
> "We may see each other ... sometime."

Charlotte:
> "No, we promised. We are both to go home."

Jerry:
> "Will it help you to know ... I'll miss you every moment?"

Charlotte:
> "So will I, Jerry. So will I."

Bette Davis as Charlotte

Paul Henreid as Jerry

Only Angels Have Wings

Burned once in love, wisecracking, devil-may-care mail pilot Geoff Carter has sworn off romance—especially when it comes to night-club entertainer Bonnie Lee, who not only can hold her own with him, but sees right through his cavalier bravado. At the tiny, isolated airstrip that Geoff calls home high in the Andes Mountains, Bonnie surprises Geoff in his cabin with a heartfelt declaration that momentarily brings the high-flying pilot down to earth.

Jean Arthur as Bonnie

Cary Grant as Geoff

Bonnie:

"Geoff, you don't have to be afraid of me anymore. I'm not trying to tie you down. I don't want to plan—I don't want to look ahead. I don't want you to change anything. I love you, Geoff. There's nothing I can do about it. I just love you, that's all. I feel the same way about you the Kid does. Anything you do is all right with me."

Geoff:

"The Kid?"

Bonnie:

"Yes, he doesn't ask you for anything, or get in your way, or bother you, does he?"

Geoff:

"Drives me nuts."
(He kisses her passionately.)

The Palm Beach Story

Practical, albeit in a loopy, decidedly mercenary fashion, Gerry Jeffers decides that the only way to bail her beloved husband, Tom, out of debt is to divorce him—and marry a rich sugar daddy to bankroll Tom's inventions. Stubbornly committed to her harebrained scheme, Gerry refuses to listen to Tom's entreaties to abandon her plan, leaving him no choice but to try a more romantic form of persuasion.

Tom: "Doesn't mean anything to you anymore to sit on my lap, huh?"

Gerry: "No."

Tom: "Or if I (kissing her back) kiss you there?"

Gerry: "Stop it, no."

Tom: "Or here (kisses her back again)."

Gerry: "It's nothing."

Tom: (wrapping arms around her) "Or here."

Gerry: (squirming) "You know I'm ticklish."

Tom: "Why's your breath coming fast?"

Gerry: "Because you're squeezing me!"
(He pulls her onto the couch and kisses her.)

Tom: "Doesn't mean anything to you anymore, huh?"

Gerry: (breathless) "Almost nothing."

Tom: "Almost nothing, huh?"
(He kisses her again, as her toes curl up.)

Claudette Colbert as Gerry

Joel McCrea as Tom

The Philadelphia Story

So imperious and judgmental that her own father suggests she might be made of bronze, Philadelphia socialite Tracy Lord finds a sympathetic ear in her supposed nemesis: *Spy Magazine* writer Macaulay "Mike" Connor, who's covering Tracy's impending nuptials, her second, for the society scandal rag. A struggling novelist slumming as a pulp journalist, Mike sees the "hearth fires" smoldering beneath Tracy's chilly veneer, as the bride-to-be and her besotted "professor" tipsily circle each other by moonlight.

Katharine Hepburn as Tracy

James Stewart as Mike

Mike: "Why, you're the golden girl, Tracy, full of life and warmth and delight. What goes on, you've got tears in your eyes?"

Tracy: "Shut up, shut up. Oh, Mike, keep talking, keep talking, talk, will you?"

Mike: (pulling away) "No, no, I've stopped."

Tracy: "Why? Has your 'mind' taken hold again, dear professor?"

Mike: "Good thing, don't you agree?"

Tracy: "No, professor."

Mike: "All right, lay off that professor stuff now, do you hear me?!"

Tracy: "Yes, professor."

Mike: "It's really all I am to you, is it?!"

Tracy: "Of course, professor."

Mike: "Are you sure?"

Tracy: "Why yes, yes, of course—" (He grabs her and kisses her passionately.)

Tracy: "Golly." (He kisses her again.)

Tracy: "Golly, Moses."

1959

Pillow Talk

She's never laid eyes on him, but Jan Morrow absolutely loathes Brad Allen, the erstwhile songwriter/full-time Lothario who ties up their shared party line, schmoozing his girlfriends du jour. Thank goodness Jan's latest squeeze, tall Texan "Rex Stetson," is nothing like that lowdown skirt-chaser Brad. Or so she thinks, for "Rex" is Brad, stepping way out of character to play Jan's gentlemanly ideal. Of course, even straitlaced types like Jan want more than a firm, hearty handshake good-night sometimes.

Doris Day as Jan

Rock Hudson as Brad

Jan:
"Well, in all the time that we've been going out together, you've been a perfect gentleman."

Brad:
"Oh, I hope I have, ma'am."

Jan:
"Well, you have. Oh, and I appreciate it, Rex, I really do. But…"

Brad:
"Yes?"

Jan:
"Well, being such a perfect gentlemen and all, it's —it's not very flattering."

Brad:
"Oh, well, ma'am, I wouldn't want to do anything that might spoil our friendship."

Jan:
"Is that all it is with us? Friendship?"

Brad:
"Ma'am, that's a direct question. I think it deserves a direct answer."
(He kisses her passionately.)

1951

A Place in the Sun

All that he's ever wanted, all that's ever eluded his desperate grasp, is now finally in reach. Poor but rabidly ambitious, factory worker George Eastman has long waited for this moment, when the bewitching, raven-haired socialite Angela Vickers falls into his arms. She is the stuff his dreams are made of: a patrician beauty with violet eyes who defies her rich parents to love a boy from the wrong side of the class divide.

Montgomery Clift as George

Elizabeth Taylor as Angela

Angela:

"If you don't come, I'll drive down to see you. I'll pick you up at the factory. You'll be my pick-up. Oh, we'll arrange it somehow, whatever way we can. We'll have such wonderful times together, just the two of us."

George:

"I'll be the happiest person in the world—."

Angela:

"The second happiest."

George:

"I can only tell you how much I love you. I can only tell you all."

Angela:

"Tell mama. Tell mama all."
(They kiss.)

The Quiet Man

Mary Kate: "Oh, but the kisses are a long way off yet!"

Sean: "Huh?"

Mary Kate: "Well, we just started a-courtin', and next month, we, we start the walkin' out, and the month after that there'll be the threshin' parties, and the month after that."

Sean: "Nope."

Mary Kate: "Well, maybe we won't have to wait that month …"

Sean: "Yup."

Mary Kate: "Or for the threshin' parties …"

Sean: "Nope."

Mary Kate: "Or for the walkin' out together."

Sean: "No."

Mary Kate: "And so much the worse for you, Sean Thornton, for I feel the same way about it myself."
(They kiss.)

Retired boxer Sean Thornton has never faced a tougher, or more beautiful, opponent than Mary Kate Danaher. He'll need a lot more than the proverbial luck of the Irish to make headway with this colleen, whose temperament matches her fiery red hair. Adamant that Sean court her in proper fashion, Mary Kate refuses to let him even think of kissing her. Then again, it is a woman's prerogative to change her mind.

Maureen O'Hara as Mary Kate

John Wayne as Sean

1952

Random Harvest

His memory a casualty of "The Great War," shell-shocked British soldier John Smith, aka "Smithy," would be lost if not for Paula. She rescued him from oblivion, taking him off the streets and away with her to a quaint village in the countryside. There they can begin a new life together, this man with no past and the compassionate music-hall entertainer who vows she'll never let him wander out of his sight.

Paula:
> "Smithy, you do mean it? You do want it? Really?"

Smithy:
> "More than anything else in the world. My life began with you. I can't imagine a future without you."

Paula:
> "Oh, I better say yes quickly, before you change your mind. It's yes, darling."

Smithy:
> "Oh, oh, now, now, I can relax!" (lying back on ground). "Hmm, I'm hungry!"

Paula:
> "Smithy?"

Smithy:
> "What is it?"

Paula:
> "Well darling, you proposed to me, and I've accepted you."

Smithy:
> "What's wrong? What's wrong?"

Paula:
> "Smithy, do I always have to take the initiative? You're supposed to kiss me, darling."

Smithy:
> (taking her in his arms) "Oh, my…"
> (He kisses her.)

Ronald Colman as Smithy

Greer Garson as Paula

Rebel Without a Cause

James Dean as Jim

Natalie Wood as Judy

Lying next to him in the shadowy ruin of an abandoned Los Angeles mansion, Judy tenderly nuzzles his cheek. Just twenty-four hours ago, when he'd shyly introduced himself to her before school, Judy had sneered at Jim's fumbling attempts at conversation and branded him "a real yo-yo." Now, after all they've been through together since that inauspicious first meeting, she can't imagine ever being apart from Jim, this troubled, sensitive boy of fierce integrity and quiet strength who's not afraid to be vulnerable.

Jim:

"We're not gonna be lonely anymore. Ever, ever. Not you or me."

Judy:

(nuzzling him) "I love somebody. All the time I've been looking for someone to love me. And now I love somebody. And it's so easy. Why is it so easy now?"

Jim:

"I don't know. Is for me, too."

Judy:

"I love you, Jim. I really mean it." (They kiss.)

Rocky

Adrian:

"I'm not sure I know you well enough. I don't feel comfortable."

Rocky:

"Yo, Adrian, you know, I ain't so comfortable either—."

Adrian:

"I should go—."

Rocky:

"Don't go, please, don't go, don't go….Do me a favor?"

Adrian:

"What?"

Rocky:

"Take off these glasses." (he removes them) "You got nice eyes. Do me another favor? Take off that hat." (he pulls off her cap.)

Rocky:

"I always know you were pretty."

Adrian:

"Don't tease me—."

Rocky:

"I'm not teasing you. I ain't teasing you. I wanna kiss you. You don't have to kiss me back, if you don't want … but I wanna kiss you." (He gently kisses her cheek, and then her mouth, as she tentatively responds.)

Nobody ever mistook him for Prince Charming, this sleepy-eyed, gentle giant of a washed-up prizefighter living hand-to-mouth in a squalid Philadelphia apartment. He can't woo her with love sonnets, take her to a fancy restaurant, or buy her a dozen red roses. All that Rocky Balboa can do is offer his lonely heart to mousy wallflower Adrian Pennino, the pet-store clerk he's been thinking about since she sold him his two pet turtles, Cuff and Link.

Talia Shire as Adrian

Sylvester Stallone as Rocky

Roman Holiday

Taking the maxim "When in Rome, do as the Romans do" impulsively to heart, Princess Anne trades her tiara for a gamine haircut and ditches her stuffy royal handlers to wander in happy anonymity through the seven hills of Rome. Savoring the simple, everyday pleasures commoners take for granted, she finds a chivalrous tour guide in handsome American journalist Joe Bradley, who plays along with her charade, until duty beckons Princess Anne to shed her disguise—and bid her heartsick lover a tearful good-bye.

Audrey Hepburn as Princess Anne

Gregory Peck as Joe

Princess Anne:

"I have to leave you now. I'm going to that corner there and turn. You must stay in the car and drive away. Promise not to watch me go beyond the corner. Just drive away and leave me—as I leave you."

Joe:

"All right."

Princess Anne:

"I don't know how to say goodbye. I can't think of any words."

Joe:

"Don't try."
(They fall into each other's arms and kiss.)

1953

1968

Romeo and Juliet

By "love's light wings" Romeo has soared over the walls into the Capulet orchard, tempting death to steal another look at Juliet, the "sun" who illuminates his heart. Though their families be locked in a violent blood-feud that's held Verona captive for years, the teenaged lovers meet in secret on Juliet's balcony, where she asks her besotted swain from the rival House of Montague to pledge his undying love.

Romeo:

"Lady, by yonder blessed moon, I swear."

Juliet:

"Oh, swear not by the moon, th'inconstant moon, that monthly changes in her circled orb, lest that thy love prove likewise variable."

Romeo:

"What shall I swear by?"

Juliet:

"Do not swear at all. Or if thou wilst…Swear by thy gracious self, which is the god of my idolatry, and I'll believe thee."

Romeo:

"If my heart's dear love, I swear! Oh, Juliet!"
(They kiss.)

Juliet:

"Sweet good night. This bud of love by summer's ripening breath may prove a beauteous flower when next we meet."
(She kisses him tenderly.)

Juliet:

"Good night, good night. As sweet repose and rest come to thy heart as that within my breast."

Olivia Hussey as Juliet

Leonard Whiting as Romeo

1998

Shakespeare in Love

In the beautiful Viola, young Will Shakespeare has found his muse. She is that profound and abiding love who inspires him to rediscover his gift for poetry. Sadly, their romance is fleeting, "like a riot in the heart." Stealing a last kiss before Viola leaves for faraway Virginia, the lovers pledge their undying devotion to one another.

Shall I compare thee to a summer's day?
Thou art more lovely and more temperate...
—William Shakespeare

Will:
> "You will never age for me.
> Nor fade—or die."

Viola:
> "Nor you for me."

Joseph Fiennes as Will Shakespeare

Gwyneth Paltrow as Viola de Lesseps

1959

Some Like It Hot

Shimmering, in a diaphanous dress that clings to her voluptuous figure, Sugar pulls "Junior" close for a deep, lingering kiss. Little does she know that he's merely feigning indifference to enflame her desire. That everything about "Junior"—the yacht, the fortune, the thick glasses—is a fraud, carefully orchestrated to turn Joe, a penniless saxophone player, into Sugar's ideal man.

Tony Curtis as Joe

Marilyn Monroe as Sugar

Sugar:

"You're not giving yourself a chance. Don't fight it. Relax…"
(She kisses him.)

Joe:

(shaking his head) "Like smoking without inhaling."

Sugar:

"So inhale!"

Joe:

"I've got a funny sensation in my toes, like someone was barbecuing them over a slow flame."

Sugar:

"Let's throw another log on the fire."
(She kisses him.)

Joe:

"I think you're on the right track."

Sugar:

"I must be. Your glasses are beginning to steam up."

1955

Summertime

He is why she's scrimped and saved her pennies all these years to make her first trip abroad: the suave, darkly handsome Italian man whose unwavering gaze holds the long-awaited promise of romance for lonely middle-aged secretary Jane Hudson. Wooing her *sotto voce*, middle-aged Venetian shopkeeper Renato Di Rossi would be the prim, Midwestern spinster's fantasy made flesh—if only he weren't married. Propriety, however, doesn't stand a chance against passion in Venice, the city of lovers.

Jane: "It's very late. We ought to go. Are you asleep?"

Renato: "Fast asleep."

Jane: "You slept all day yesterday."

Renato: "True."

Jane: "You sleep all day, and then you don't want to sleep at night." (They kiss.)

Jane: "You promised to take me to see the lacemaking, and now it's too late."

Renato: "I will take you tomorrow."

Jane: "You promise?"

Renato: (smiling) "No." (They kiss.)

Jane: "Now do you promise?"

Renato: "That makes it more difficult."

Jane: "If you don't take me, I'll never kiss you again."

Renato: "Yes, you will."

Jane: "Yes, I guess I will." (They kiss.)

Rosanno Brazzi as Renato

Katharine Hepburn as Jane

Terms of Endearment

Her dignity scattered to the wind, along with her expensive head scarf and what's left of her reputation, uptight Houston widow Aurora Greenway rues the day she ever invited neighbor Garrett Breedlove to lunch. A boozy, unrepentant womanizer with a devilish grin and roaming hands, he shocks and offends Aurora right down to her starchy, ultra-controlling core. All the more reason to invite him over later that very night to see her Renoir painting, which incidentally hangs in her bedroom.

Garrett:

"Hi…I was doing laps when you called. Lucky for us, only did eight."

Aurora:

"This is it. This is the Renoir."

Garrett:

(putting arm around her) "Like it. Like the painting. I like everything in here. Relax, baby, it's gonna be great."

Aurora:

(pulling away) "Just who do you think you're talking to like this? Don't you realize I'm a grandmother?!"
(She grabs him and kisses him hungrily.)

Shirley MacLaine as Aurora

Jack Nicholson as Garrett

1983

The Thin Man

Never one to let a little thing like murder interfere with his drinking, retired gumshoe Nick Charles would much rather spend his days getting soused than solving crimes. Rarely at a loss for a quip or a martini, he's found his chic, quick-witted foil in the lovely Nora, who's quite the detective herself. When not downing cocktails or hurling good-natured barbs at each other, the gin-soaked soul mates find time to crack the occasional murder case—and pucker up for a red-hot kiss.

Nora: "Go on, see if I care. But I think it's a dirty trick to bring me all the way to New York, just to make a widow of me."

Nick: "You wouldn't be a widow long."

Nora: "You bet I wouldn't."

Nick: "Not with all your money."
(He tries to kiss her, but she turns away.)

Nick: "Any port in a storm. Good-bye, sugah!"

Nora: "Nicky! Nicky!"

Nick: "Hmm?"

Nora: "Take care of yourself."

Nick: (chortling) "Oh, sure I will."

Nora: "Don't say it like that. Say it as if you meant it."

Nick: "Well, I do believe the little woman cares."

Nora: "I don't care. It's just that I'm used to you, that's all."
(She grabs him with a kiss.)

Myrna Loy as Nora

William Powell as Nick

Titanic

They never should have met. He's a scrappy charmer who won a steerage ticket in a poker game. She's a Philadelphia Main Line beauty with a good name but no money, traveling first-class with her mother and wealthy cad of a fiancé. On the maiden voyage of the grandest ocean liner the world's ever seen, Jack Dawson and Rose DeWitt-Bukater connect with one lingering glance. And from that moment on, nothing will separate Rose from Jack, the boy who teaches her how to fly on the prow of the *HMS Titanic*.

Leonardo DiCaprio as Jack

Kate Winslet as Rose

Jack:

"Give me your hand. Now close your eyes. Go on. Step up. Now hold onto the railing. Keep your eyes closed; don't peek."

Rose:

"I'm not."

Jack:

"Step up onto the rail. Hold on. Hold on. Keep your eyes closed. Do you trust me?"

Rose:

"I trust you."

Jack:

"All right, open your eyes."

Rose:

"I'm flying! Jack!"

Jack:

(singing softly) "Come Josephine, my flying machine, going up, she goes, up, she goes …" (They kiss.)

To Catch a Thief

Once a thief, always a thief. At least that's what gorgeous, thrill-seeking socialite Frances Stevens believes, and avidly hopes, about John Robie, alias "The Cat," despite his claims of being retired. As fireworks blaze and crackle in the night sky outside her luxurious French Riviera hotel suite, illuminating the diamond necklace around her elegant neck, Frances tempts John out of his retirement—to steal a kiss.

Frances:

"Look, John. Diamonds. The only thing in the world you can't resist. Then tell me you don't know what I'm talking about."
(She kisses his fingers.)

Frances:

"Never had a better offer in your whole life. One with everything."

John:

"I never had a crazier one."

Frances:

"Just as long as you're satisfied."

John:

"You know as well as I do this necklace is imitation."

Frances:

"Well, I'm not."
(They kiss.)

Cary Grant as John

Grace Kelly as Frances

To Have and Have Not

He thought he'd seen it all until she slinked her way into his fleabag hotel room—a sloe-eyed, light-fingered dame with a heart of brass and a mouth to match. A hard-drinking charter boat captain, navigating his way through the treacherous waters off World War II–era Martinique, Harry's got enough on his hands, what with smuggling French resistance fighters past the Vichy police, to get all hot and bothered with "Slim," who insists on calling him Steve. But that was before she taught him how to whistle.

Lauren Bacall as Slim

Humphrey Bogart as Harry

Slim:
> "You know, Steve, you're not very hard to figure. Only at times. Sometimes I know exactly what you're going to say—most of the time. The other times …"
> (She slides onto his lap.)

Slim:
> "The other times you're just a stinker."
> (She kisses him.)

Harry:
> "What'd you do that for?"

Slim:
> "Been wondering whether I'd like it."

Harry:
> "What's the decision?"

Slim:
> "I don't know yet."
> (She kisses him again—he pulls her closer to him.)

Slim:
> "It's even better when you help."

Two for the Road

You couldn't ask for a more romantic getaway than a seaside hilltop in the South of France. For the moment, however, all this astonishing natural beauty is lost on Mark and Joanna, whose idyllic swim in the Mediterranean has abruptly dissolved in a nasty quarrel. Such is the pattern of their intensely mercurial but fiercely loving bond, forged while hitchhiking together across France—and playing out, once again, as he chases her up the hillside path.

Joanna: "I never want to see you again—."

Mark: "Not much (stubbing toe). Ow!"

Joanna: "As long as I live!"

Mark: "Joanna!"

Joanna: "No!"

Mark: "I've decided we should get married! What do you say?"

Joanna: (rushing back to him) "Yes!" (They kiss.)

Joanna: "I won't ever let you down."

Mark: "I will you."

Joanna: "I don't care what you do, just as long as I've got you."

Mark: "Hmm, Joanna Wallace."

Joanna: "You won't be sorry, sir."

Mark: "You will."

Joanna: "Never. Never, never, never, never…" (They kiss.)

Albert Finney as Mark

Audrey Hepburn as Joanna

1964

The Umbrellas of Cherbourg

Two years—that's how long Guy will be away from her, fighting in the Algerian War. The thought of being apart from him even one day, much less two years, is more than heartsick Geneviève can bear. In the all-consuming throes of first love, the gorgeous seventeen-year-old shop girl clings to the handsome garage mechanic, bidding him a tearful farewell on their last night together in the seaside Normandy village of Cherbourg.

Nino Castelnuovo as Guy

Catherine Deneuve as Geneviève

Guy:

"We have so little time left. So little time, my love, and we musn't waste it. We must try to be happy. Of our last moments we must keep a memory more beautiful than anything. A memory to help us live."

Geneviève:

"I'm so afraid when I'm alone."

Guy:

"We'll be together again, and we'll be stronger."

Geneviève:

"You'll meet other women—you'll forget me."

Guy:

"I will love you until the end of my life."

Geneviève:

"Guy, I love you. Don't leave me!"
(They kiss.)

Every day he watches her—and every day he falls more in love with the enigmatic, ice-cool blonde he's been hired to follow, as she winds her way through San Francisco to the grave of a long-dead Spanish woman. Obsessed with the otherworldly, suicidal Madeline, private investigator Scottie Ferguson abandons all reason to plunge headlong into a dizzying, passionate romance with the haunted beauty.

Vertigo

Madeline:

"Oh, Scottie, I'm not mad, I'm not mad! I don't want to die. There's someone within me, and she says I must die. Oh, Scottie, don't let me go."

Scottie:

"I'm here. I've got you."

Madeline:

"I'm so afraid."
(They kiss.)

Madeline:

"Don't leave me. Stay with me."

Scottie:

"All the time."
(He kisses her again.)

Kim Novak as Madeline

James Stewart as Scottie

West Side Story

Their eyes meet across a crowded dance floor—as everything around them magically fades to black, transforming a dingy, neighborhood gym into an enchanted meeting place for star-crossed lovers. In an instant, they escape the harsh reality of the New York streets—where a violent feud between rival gangs conspires to keep a Puerto Rican girl and a Polish-American boy forever apart—to share "one hand, one heart"... and a sweet first kiss.

Tony:
"You're ... not thinking I'm someone else?"

Maria:
"I know you are not."

Tony:
"Or that we've met before?"

Maria:
"I know we have not."

Tony:
"I felt ... I knew something never before was gonna happen—had to happen, but this is so much more."

Maria:
"My hands are cold."(taking his hands)
"Yours, too." (she caresses his face) "So warm."

Tony:
(touching her face) "So beautiful."

Maria:
"Beautiful."

Tony:
"So much to believe. You're not making a joke?"

Maria:
"I have not yet learned how to joke that way. I think now I never will."

Richard Beymer as Tony

Natalie Wood as Maria

When Harry Met Sally

Can men and women be "just friends," without sex entering the picture? The answer to the age-old question would appear to be a resounding, vehement "no" for Harry Burns and Sally Albright, whose long-in-the-works, carefully cultivated, supposedly platonic relationship ends in bitterness and tears after spending the night together. Then again, who better to marry than a friend who not only tolerates your many quirks and neuroses, but loves them?

Billy Crystal as Harry

Meg Ryan as Sally

Harry:

"I love that after I spend a day with you, I can still smell your perfume on my clothes. And I love that you are the last person I want to talk to before I go to sleep at night. And it's not because I'm lonely, and it's not because it's New Year's Eve. I came here tonight, because when you realize you want to spend the rest of your life with somebody, you want the rest of your life to start as soon as possible."

Sally:

"You see? That is just like you, Harry. You say things like that, and you make it impossible for me to hate you! And I hate you, Harry. I really hate … hate you." (They kiss.)

Woman of the Year

Waging the battle of the sexes in dueling newspaper columns, globetrotting foreign correspondent Tess Harding and down-to-earth sportswriter Sam Craig are a classic case of opposites attract. If she's like a fine wine, made from grapes cultivated in an ancient vineyard, then he'd be an ice-cold bottle of nickel beer, served up at Yankee stadium. Well-lubricated after a round of cocktails, they declare a truce that brings their war of words to a sweet close.

Katharine Hepburn as Tess

Spencer Tracy as Sam

Tess: (eyes shut) "This is good."

Sam: (pulling her head onto his chest) "This is better. Tess?"

Tess: "Hmm?"

Sam: "There's something I've got to get off my chest."

Tess: (lifting her head) "I'm too heavy?"

Sam: "No."

Tess: "Then what?"

Sam: "I love you."

Tess: "You do?

Sam: "Positive."

Tess: "That's nice. Even when I'm sober?"

Sam: "Even when you're brilliant."
(They kiss.)

Acknowledgments

I received invaluable advice and assistance from many people while working on this book. First and foremost, I am especially grateful to Les Krantz, my longtime mentor and frequent collaborator, whose guidance and persistence made *Great Kisses* possible. Thanks also to Sarah Durand, my astute editor at HarperCollins, and her crackerjack editorial assistant, Emily Krump. And to Kris Grauvogl and Leslie Gostomski of Nei-Turner Media Group, for their design expertise. Finally, I'd like to thank the following people for their film suggestions and unfailing support: Jack Bennett, Tina Curran, Katie Gates, Steve Kadel, Jeffrey & Sheila Lane, Rick Nahmias, and Don Shenk.